Belgian Tervuren

Training Secrets

Mark Mendoza

Contents

Belgian Tervuren Breed Profile

The Belgian Tervuren is an active and intelligent member of the Herding Group. These dogs were bred to guard and herd livestock, with the physical appearance to prove it, showing off a proud posture and an elegantly muscular body. It combines great strength with agility and speed, and has the energy to run and herd non-stop all day.

The temperament of the Belgian Tervuren is as playful and alert as any breed, yet will turn quickly to reserved and defensive around strange people. They are natural watchdogs and fearless protectors. These dogs function best when ongoing mental stimulation and training is followed. They are well-mannered in the house and are safe around children, with the exception of minor nipping in the attempt to herd them.

A Brief History Of The Belgian Tervuren

The Belgian Tervuren has its roots in Belgium and has been around since the 1800s. This dog is actually one of four Belgian dog breeds. All four share the same origins, with the major distinction being the coat type and color patterns. They are the long, black haired Groenendael, the short haired Malinois, the wire haired Laekenois, and the non-black haired Tervuren.

All of these breeds were used as herding dogs and as guard dogs, and were interbred both before and after being officially organized into one breed, known as the Continental or the Belgian. The Tervuren was named after a small village, known as the village of Tervuren, where the dog had its earlier residences. They were not quite as popular as the other shepherd breeds but still made the official AKC registration list in the United States in 1918.

Upkeep Requirements For The Belgian Tervuren

The Belgian Tervuren, like all breeds from the Herding Group, must have lots of daily exercise. Strenuous activity in the form of running and outside games are best. They are easily trained and thrive on mental stimulation as well. They specifically enjoy herding and will even attempt to herd small children if left unsupervised.

These dogs have tolerance to moderately cool and warm temperatures, and should be given the room to roam outside during the day. Belgian Tervuren dogs absolutely cannot live in a small, closed-in space. Although they do thrive on human companionship and contact, they need plenty of time outdoors. Grooming requirements for the dog's double coat needs a good brushing, two to three times per week.

Health Concerns

The average lifespan of the Belgian Tervuren is between ten and twelve years. Major health concerns that are commonly seen in the breed are seizures. Minor health issues include PRA, hypothyroidism, allergies, CHD, and elbow dysplasia. Rarely seen is hemangiosarcoma, pannus, PPM, and cataracts. Veterinarians suggest that the Belgian Tervuren get specifically tested for eye, hip, and elbow problems.

Obedience Training: A Belgian Tervuren Owner's Guide

A lot of dog owners often complain about their Belgian Tervuren's uncontrollable behavior and find themselves at a loss as to how to properly teach their highly spirited canines some manners. The inability of dogs to learn simple commands such as 'sit' and 'stay' can crucially become a major problem in the future with the possibility of your once pesky dog to become a family pest or even worse a neighborhood nuisance. Hence, it makes it all the more imperative for Belgian Tervuren owners to teach their precious dogs obedience lessons before it's too late.

Obedience training, in essence should not be treated as a means to teach your Belgian Tervuren to do fancy tricks or perform competition exercises. The main premise of obedience training is to simply teach obedience and basically teach them to follow simple commands. Before anything else, family should be carefully inculcated to your Belgian Tervuren, as this will vitally ensure harmonious cohabitation for years.

While other dog owners prefer to send their dogs to obedience classes, any dedicated dog lover can actually do this at the comforts of their own home. This will provide more time for the dog and the owner to bond and improve their communication skills. Obedience training basically requires a healthy dose of patience, a collar and a leash, lots of sense of humor and a keen understanding to the natural Belgian Tervuren behavior. For people who never had any prior experience with raising dogs, it might be more helpful to read books about the particular breed they own to fully grasp the dog's behavior.

Age Matters

So what would be the best time for train your Belgian Tervuren?

Experts claim that's its highly recommended to train them as early as 8 weeks old. The old adage "you can't teach old dogs new tricks" may have a grain of truth to it, to some extent. This is mainly because like human beings, as dogs age the mental abilities also diminishes, which predictably have a great impact on efficacy of the training. It is also said that after three months, dogs have more or less established their unique behavior that can be quite hard to eliminate in place of newer ones.

Understanding the Canine Psyche and Learning Styles

The unique about dogs is the fact that unlike the other members in the animal kingdom, canines take more pleasure in learning and performing. Of course, the level of intelligence vary from certain breeds, but more often than not dogs in general display a better response in learning new things. For Belgian Tervuren owners, it can be equally stimulating and a thoroughly enjoyable experience.

However, don't fall in the mistake of assuming that training dogs as similar to teaching children. This is simply not the case. Why? For one, canines are entirely different specie and their differences from man doesn't' just end in the physical aspect. Keep in mind that things are wholly different from your dogs' point of view. Dogs have limited field of vision, which can be a hindrance in the obedience training. While we can easily see objects on a seemingly bird's eye view, your dogs line of vision are what might seems like cluttered objects, such as chairs and doors they cannot open.

Another important thing to keep in mind is the fact that dogs have a keen sense of smell and hearing, which can play a major advantage in calling out commands as well as become a source of distractions too. While you are busy teaching your Belgian Tervuren, he may pick on certain sounds such as the starting of a car engine, which definitely poses as a major diversion. The great thing is if you have a treat well hidden in your pocket, your dog can easily pick out that smell; this can undoubtedly work on your advantage and cajole him in becoming more attentive.

In fully understand the canine psyche, humans have to acknowledge can dogs too know how to communicate – albeit in an entirely different language. So if you pay careful attention to their barks, whines, yowls and growls you can more or else distinguish and understand what they want to tell you. The different sounds they make are usually good indicator of their mood and any other form of expression.

Like pre-school children, dogs often display an adorable eagerness to learn. They may not appear to prefer what you teach them, but at they end of the day they will be able to pick out a thing or two after every training session.

Training Basics

The basic requirement for obedience training is a six-foot leash made of either nylon or leather. Experts don't usually recommend the use flexi or retractable leases for training. You will also need a sturdy collar that should be fitted properly. Always keep handy some treats or toys to use as reward for your dogs and lots of water, too. For Belgian Tervuren owners, you need to have a steady stream of patience coupled with a highly positive attitude. Dogs can sense your moods, whether you are tense or properly relaxed, and will predictably respond accordingly.

It is equally important to choose the area that has limited distractions so your Belgian Tervuren will find it easier to focus on whatever task at hand. Keep in mind that the younger the Belgian Tervuren, the shorter should be the training session. A typical session should be a maximum of two to three sessions in a day and each session should not exceed more than five to ten minutes in length. If you notice that your Belgian Tervuren is not feeling well, schedule the training session for later as this will only give you and your Belgian Tervuren a hard time. Some experts recommend training dogs when they are hungry mainly because you can easily use food treats as reinforcements. This state, your Belgian Tervuren will considerably be more agile and more willing to please.

Basic Commands

Sit/Stay – for this session, your Belgian Tervuren should be on a leash in front of you. Carefully hold a treat above his head and give the command in a clear voice 'sit'. By forcing your Belgian Tervuren to look up to the treat, he will need to sit on his rear end. Then slowly the treat in the direction of his tail to force him to adapt a complete sitting position. Be ready to repeat this command several times until such time your Belgian Tervuren will sit properly. Do not forget to provide rewards and praise whenever he responds correctly.

Come – This command should be taught early in order for your Belgian Tervuren to easily recall this particular order all throughout his lifetime. Treats are also used to lure your Belgian Tervuren to come to you. Start with placing a dry food on a plastic container then show it to your Belgian Tervuren while clearly saying the word 'treat'. This will help your Belgian Tervuren associate the sound of shakers (meat in plastic) with treats. Do this as often as needed until such time your Belgian Tervuren will visibly respond to the sound of the shaker.

After a few sessions use the shaker to call him towards you. But this time be sure to call out the word 'come' before using the shaker. If your Belgian Tervuren responds correctly, give him a treat. In time your Belgian Tervuren will learn to associate the word come with a shaker, that's the only time you start to gradually increase your distance. Make sure that you will not call your Belgian Tervuren to reprimand him, as this will only cause negative reactions every time you call him in the future.

Down – begin with your Belgian Tervuren on a sitting position and use the treat to lure him to bend halfway to the ground. Slowly move your hand closer to the ground and once he starts to understand, gently move the food away. Do this for several repetitions until he can easily move his head towards the ground. After having achieved that, try to move the lure under his chest and wait for a few seconds. At this point, would readily learn to drop. Exercise later without the bait to get him to cooperate.

Heel – for dog owners, it can be quite exasperating to have an untrained Belgian Tervuren on a leash moving along a very busy sidewalk. It can be a perfect recipe for disaster, especially if there is another Belgian Tervuren in sight. Untrained dogs are more likely to crisscross, trip other people and practically become a walking pest and peril. Teaching your dog to heel is one of the most essential commands in order to instill some disciple especially if you are out on public.

Like other commands, this is taught using a leash. From the sit/stay position, allow your Belgian Tervuren to warm up by giving him free rein to rum. Then command him to sit/stay on your left side and firmly grasp the leash halfway between the Belgian Tervuren and your right hand. This will provide you a corrective hold when needed. Call out clearly the command 'Heel!' with the Belgian Tervuren's name. For example, "Hell, Chuck!' As you give out the command, move with your left foot first. Your Belgian Tervuren will either dash forward or lag behind. These are among the expected reactions. This is when you need to make some corrective and instantaneous reactions. If he tries to dash, let him do so but only until at the need of the leash, then yank hard. Walk up to him and command 'sit/stay', then praise or pat him on the head. If he lags behind, don't try to drag him but instead wait for him to come along with you, gently using the leash to urge him on, then make him sit or stay. Do not forget to praise him or give the reward after every command.

Once your Belgian Tervuren learns how to heel with the leash, teach him to be on a sitting position once you stop walking. Walking him in a short distance, then stop and give out the heel command or signal him to sit. You need to keep repeating this walk and sit routine until such time you need not call out a command but simply use hand signals.

Rewards and Reprimands

The most important part of any obedience training is providing rewards to your Belgian Tervuren on an especially good and Cooperative behavior. Studies have shown that rewards promote quicker learning methods as food being considered as the primary incentive. It is therefore important all throughout the obedience training to repeatedly set situations to practice and get treats as rewards. Praise and reward are important to always maintaining proper Belgian Tervuren behavior and prevent attitude problems from arising in the future.

In their daily lives, dogs are often bombarded with stringent commands such as 'NO', 'STOP', 'BAD Belgian Tervuren, which ultimately tends to become meaningless and are often ignored. Whenever you find the great need to reprimand your Belgian Tervuren, it would be a more effective approach to show him immediately what you want him to do and reward him if he gets it right. That would be a more constructive approach. For example, if you find him gnawing at a piece of your furniture, tell him 'OFF' right away, and immediately lead him to his toys and encourage him to chew on them instead. Don't forget to praise him or give a treat for doing so.

If a reprimand is done correctly, your voice will be sufficient enough as a command. The best way to address a reprimand is to keep it short, sharp and immediate. It would prove to be quite futile to nag at your Belgian Tervuren, as they will not understand you at all. Never reprimand him if you don't actually catch him on the act.

A lot of animal experts adamantly discourage hitting, slapping, kicking or spanking dog dogs. This is simply an inappropriate punishment and will only create more problems or worsen existing problems in the future. You wouldn't want your Belgian Tervuren to grow overly timid or fearful, right?

A Lifetime Commitment

Every dog owner should rightfully acknowledge that learning for dogs that not simply end in a few weeks of training classes. It should be a life long learning experience both for the Belgian Tervuren and the dog owner. Raising a Belgian Tervuren should be viewed as a start of a wonderful friendship, and your dog should be treated with love and respect accordingly. By properly reinforcing rewards and praise, you will effectively be able to promote good behavior at the same time bond with your dog. Most dogs naturally sense and acknowledge humans as their superior. In response, people as dog owners should be able to willingly take on the responsibility and provide consistent leadership and guidance. Raising a Belgian Tervuren is indeed a lifetime commitment and should be given much consideration and deliberation for the whole family. Every member should take part in training the Belgian Tervuren and making it a highly welcome addition in the household.

How to Stop the 10 Most Common Belgian Tervuren Obedience Problems

Every Belgian Tervuren owner has been down this road before – the head banging futility of trying to teach your Belgian Tervuren, whether young or old, how to overcome a particular behavior problem. Unfortunately, in some cases it can be downright impossible to get through to them and overcome whatever mental blocks and obedience issues they have.

There are a variety of reasons this could be. Your Belgian Tervuren may have entirely too much energy, the result of not getting enough exercise. Your Belgian Tervuren might be challenging your position as the alpha leader of the household – something that needs to be nipped in the bud immediately to avoid potentially worse problems. Or your Belgian Tervuren just may never have been given specific boundaries to follow.

Whatever is causing your Belgian Tervuren's obedience problems, know that 99.9% of all dogs are good at heart and capable of learning exactly how to behave. It's only a matter of finding the teaching method that works for them and being consistent in how you approach their issues.

That's why you're reading this; to find out what your Belgian Tervuren wants and needs to see and hear from you to avoid the negative impact of these behaviors in your home. So, let's get started and take a look at how you can curb everything from a leaky bladder to flat out aggression.

1. Potty Issues

When it comes to a Belgian Tervuren's bladder, there are many potential problems. It is not always an immediate issue of a Belgian Tervuren not wanting to go outside – sometimes it is a matter of them not being able to hold it that long or simply not understanding the boundaries between inside and outside.

In reality, the last thing a Belgian Tervuren wants to do is go to the bathroom in their home. They are hardwired to go away from their dens, to avoid the impact of disease and parasites that can plague them in the wild. This is one of the primary reasons a Belgian Tervuren will hold their urine for so long when you leave the house – they don't want to make a mess in their home.

The real issue comes in when a) the Belgian Tervuren doesn't understand that the house is their home and is not trained to tell the difference and b) when the Belgian Tervuren is not taken outside often enough to relieve itself. So, the first thing we need to do is determine which category your Belgian Tervuren falls into and what the quickest and easiest way to solve the problem is.

Consistency and Small Breeds

Assuming a Belgian Tervuren has been at least partially housebroken, the first thing you need to ask yourself is whether the Belgian Tervuren is being taken outside often enough. This comes up most commonly with small breeds like pinschers, Yorkshire terriers, dachshunds, or pugs – dogs that have small bladders and minimal insulation. When the weather gets cold or wet, owners will often times minimize the amount of time they submit their dogs to the elements. They figure that allowing their Belgian Tervuren to make a small mess inside won't hurt them and it is easy to clean up.

Unfortunately, while a single mess might not seem like a big deal at the time, it can actually cause a number of problems further down the line. To start with, the Belgian Tervuren does not want to go to the bathroom inside – especially if it has been trained to go outside. It is their home and they are more comfortable going outside. Imagine how comfortable you would be relieving yourself in the kitchen sink instead of in the bathroom.

Secondly, a Belgian Tervuren that is allowed to make a mess inside will never learn that the bathroom is outdoors. Dogs do not have a natural inclination to delineate between indoor and outdoor areas. You need to teach them.

Handling Potty Problems

If your Belgian Tervuren makes messes on the floor, the easiest thing to do is to start from scratch. Crate training is a very effective tool because it gives the Belgian Tervuren a smaller space to claim as their own, tapping into that instinctual desire to not make a mess where they sleep. If crate training is out of the question, you should confine the Belgian Tervuren to a single room and pay close attention to them. Create a routine that allows the Belgian Tervuren to go to the bathroom at the same time every day, and when the Belgian Tervuren does their business outdoors, make sure to praise them profusely. On the flip side, do not get angry if your Belgian Tervuren makes a mess inside.

Attempt to startle them with a sharp noise, such as clapping your hands, and then take them outside immediately so they begin associating outdoors with relieving themselves. Just remember that punishing your Belgian Tervuren for making a mess will have no impact. The Belgian Tervuren is incapable of understanding why they are being punished before they fully understand that they are not permitted to go to the bathroom indoors.

Additionally, it is a good idea to have your carpets thoroughly cleaned to remove any dog odor that may linger. Conventional cleaners tend to just mask the smell to human noses. Dogs, on the other hand, can still smell their markings and will return there later. If you have more than one Belgian Tervuren, they may even attempt to mark over the top of each other, leading to a cycle that can be hard to break.

2. Aggression Problems

There is nothing more alarming than a Belgian Tervuren with aggression problems. Such issues can be a sign of a number of problems. If you adopted your Belgian Tervuren as an adult, they may have been poorly treated as a Belgian Tervuren. If you raised the Belgian Tervuren without proper limits, they may be trying to assert dominance over those around them. If the Belgian Tervuren is bored or has excess energy they may have developed anxiety or fear issues that need to be assuaged by strong, alpha leadership.

This is a hard one to provide specific advice on, because all dogs are different and each aggressive tendency needs to be handled with special care and specific actions according to the Belgian Tervuren and their issues. In many cases, it is a good idea to hire a Belgian Tervuren training or behavior specialist who can help outline a plan to treat your Belgian Tervuren's aggression. For general issues, however, here are some tips to get you started.

Pinpointing Sources of Aggression

To start with, you need to determine what is causing your Belgian Tervuren's aggressive behavior. Some people may not catch the patterns until they stop and check it directly. Here are some common aggression issues that you may encounter:

- Food Aggression
- Towards Children

- Towards other Dogs

- Towards Strangers

Once you've distinguished what is causing the aggression in your Belgian Tervuren, it is time to avoid those particular situations as much as possible for the foreseeable future. If your Belgian Tervuren is aggressive towards other dogs, don't take them to a Belgian Tervuren park until you can determine if the behavior is curable. The same goes toward children and food. While addressing an aggression issue, it is extremely important to be careful.

Positive Reinforcement

The majority of training regiments will include positive reinforcement – the process of providing treats and praise to a Belgian Tervuren when they act as you want them to act. One common way to do this is to have your Belgian Tervuren on a leash and stand far away from the source of aggression. Give your Belgian Tervuren treats and praise and then move closer to the source of aggression. They will eventually start to see that source of aggression as a source of reward and get excited rather than angry when they see it.

The important thing to remember here is that your Belgian Tervuren will not react well to negative reinforcement. Punishment will escalate and can result in aggression or violence. You might even cause your Belgian Tervuren to bite, as most aggression is a result of fear and anxiety – violence and anger only heighten that fear.

Additionally, never punish a Belgian Tervuren for growling. That growling is scary, but it is a warning sign of discomfort. If you remove it, your Belgian Tervuren may simply bite instead without the warning needed to remove them from the situation.

Food Aggression – If your Belgian Tervuren shows signs of food aggression, there are a few things you should do. To start with, never punish the Belgian Tervuren for that aggression. Instead, you need to retrain them to think differently. This starts by setting up a feeding schedule. Stop filling the bowl at all times, and start feeding them only 2-3 times a day with the same amount of food. By becoming the source of the food, they look to you for the food rather than attempting to protect what they feel is theirs. Additionally, you can try feeding your Belgian Tervuren in a different room to remove the sense of ownership over that location, and you should always remove any other dogs from the room and feed them separately if necessary.

Aggression with Other Dogs – Another common source of aggression is towards other dogs. If you have another Belgian Tervuren in your home, this can be resolved by going on a walk together and letting them get to know each other on leashes. If the dogs have been around each other for some time, it can be a sign that your dogs do not have a clear leader in their pack and are fighting with each other for that role. When this happens, you need to step up and take the alpha leadership position. Often times, simply by showing clear leadership, you can negate any negative behaviors in the dogs of your home towards each other.

Avoid Rewarding the Behavior – The number one thing that all Belgian Tervuren owners need to remember is that aggression is not acceptable and cannot be allowed. If your Belgian Tervuren snaps at someone, don't dog them afterwards or try to be reassuring. It will only reinstall the behavior. Don't punish them either as it can be confusing and create worse situations. Your goal should be to address correcting the behavior, not directly reacting to it.

As you can see, there are many ways a Belgian Tervuren might exhibit aggressive behavior and many ways to stall or eliminate that behavior. The one constant among it all is the need of the owner to be consistent in their actions and to provide strong, alpha leadership for the Belgian Tervuren. Training your Belgian Tervuren through obedience training is another important step as well.

If Things Go Too Far

Don't forget that there are options to help you control your Belgian Tervuren while training them. To start with, see a vet to ensure your Belgian Tervuren is in good health and their aggression is not a medical problem. Second, obtain restrictive leashes or muzzles if they are necessary in public. Finally, stop making a big deal about certain things like when another Belgian Tervuren approaches or when strangers are nearby. Your Belgian Tervuren feeds on that anxiety and will react accordingly, especially on a leash. It all starts with powerful, strong leadership from the owner. If you can provide that, your Belgian Tervuren's aggressive tendencies will be much easier to deal with.

3. Digging

Digging is one of many natural behaviors that dogs would perform in the wild. In this case, it is important because they will dig up den space for their pups and to hide food from other predators. So, when a Belgian Tervuren digs, it is because of a deep seeded need to do so. Most often, they enjoy it and at times, they can become obsessive. Digging itself is not harmful to your Belgian Tervuren – in some cases it can be therapeutic for them, if properly channelled.

Unfortunately, whether your Belgian Tervuren is getting a great deal of enjoyment out of their digging or not, they are likely destroying your flower garden or your backyard in the process. So, you'll want to find a good balance that will minimize the digging behavior without stifling your Belgian Tervuren's desire to play and use up energy.

The Root of Digging

The first thing to do is determine why your Belgian Tervuren is digging. In many cases, digging is a result of excess energy and boredom – a messy combination in many Belgian Tervuren breeds.

Common family Belgian Tervuren breeds like Labradors and Retrievers will often be full of excess energy. If they are not walked and played with often enough or if they are locked up in the backyard without anyone to keep them busy, they may turn to digging as an outlet for that excess energy. Dogs don't watch TV or read books when they're bored – they tend to destroy things, channelling their instincts into something they enjoy.

Breaking the Habit

So, before attempting to change your Belgian Tervuren's behavior, first spend some time determining what you can do to minimize the causes. Find more time to walk your Belgian Tervuren, spend some time in the backyard exercising with them, and make sure you are attending their needs at all times. If you toss your Belgian Tervuren in the backyard all day and leave them be, don't expect to find a pristine lawn when you return.

To start, protect any areas you don't want dug up. You can cover the areas that your Belgian Tervuren likes to dig with something they cannot dig through – like rocks or tarps. Your Belgian Tervuren wants soft dirt to dig up, so if you can minimize the areas that they have access to, you'll be able to cut them off easier. Another good trick is to sprinkle natural Belgian Tervuren repellents like red pepper flakes, pennyroyal oil, or citronella – all easily available.

Finally, you need to give your Belgian Tervuren something solid to think about other than the destructive behaviors they have picked up. For many high energy dogs, simple training or obedience school can help with this. Because you're giving your Belgian Tervuren commands they need to think about, you are replacing the urges and desires they have to dig with constructive actions that you can control.

Finally, if you really must leave your Belgian Tervuren in a place where they can dig excessively, provide them with a toy or an alternative way to burn off that excess energy. Toys, bones, or a second Belgian Tervuren with which to play are all good ways to reduce the un-channelled energy that gets unleashed on your poor peonies.

Creating a Special Digging Space

Another trick that works well for many Belgian Tervuren owners is to provide the Belgian Tervuren with a dedicated digging area that they are allowed to play in. Take a kiddie pool and fill it in with dirt, possibly even with Belgian Tervuren treats buried in the dirt. Then, when the Belgian Tervuren wants to dig, let them dig there. If you find them digging in your lawn at all, simply clap your hands and attain their attention. By doing this, you can claim the backyard as your space and tell your Belgian Tervuren that they are not

permitted to dig in it, but that they have their own space in the kiddie pool.

4. Barking

Every Belgian Tervuren barks occasionally – whether to exhibit excitement or to tell you they are bored. The problem is that some dogs get carried away and do not stop barking. They grow agitated at any sound they hear inside or outside the home or they simple bark for the sake of barking. In these cases, an owner will quickly grow impatient, as will their neighbours. So it is important to take action sooner than later, communicating to your Belgian Tervuren that barking is not permitted for the sake of barking.

Why Your Belgian Tervuren Barks

To start with, know that your Belgian Tervuren is likely bred to bark. Almost all breeds were bred to make noise in some form or another. Hunting dogs and terriers barked to alert their masters to the fact that they found something. Herding dogs were bred to bark and nip at the animals they were herding. Even some working dogs were bred to become vocal when necessary. And of course, dogs bark naturally as a sign of excitement or aggression. I could outline what all of our Belgian Tervuren's barks mean, but you likely have a good idea based on the tone and body language of the animal – they are just communicating.

Minimizing Barking

The real goal then, rather than stopping your Belgian Tervuren from barking completely, is to minimize that barking. There are very few situations in which your Belgian Tervuren should bark endlessly, even when communicating to you. But, at the same time, you want your Belgian Tervuren to be able to warn you if there is danger, communicate when it needs to go outside, and keep other animals away if it is uncomfortable or afraid.

Exercise – To start with, make sure your Belgian Tervuren gets the exercise it needs to release any pent up energy that could be leading to excess barking. Often times, barking can be the result of boredom or anxiety – exercise will help to reduce that.

Don't Reinforce the Behavior – The number one reason dogs continue to bark, after energy level problems, is simply that their owners reinforce the behavior. They feel bad for the Belgian Tervuren when they whine or simply want them to stop barking when they are angry. So, they give them attention, give them their food, or take them outside. Your goal should be to never give your Belgian Tervuren what they want when they bark. If you need to wait them out, do it – giving them what they want when they bark at you will only teach them to continue doing it.

Anger and Shouting Causes Confusion – Yelling at your Belgian Tervuren or getting angry will only cause confusion. As with most behavior, they don't know they're doing something wrong, and they will only get confused if you start yelling at them. Along these same lines, avoid any punishment laden treatments like shock collars. They are inhumane and most dogs will try to learn how to get around them.

Training – Simple training can be very helpful in minimizing barking behavior in your Belgian Tervuren. Teach them to sit, lie down, or shake as well as to speak and be quiet. These simple commands cause them to shift focus to you and away from whatever they are barking about. Additionally, teaching them to bark and stop barking on command gives you more control over their vocal habits.

Controlling their Outdoor Behaviors – If your Belgian Tervuren barks continuously outside, they will never learn to stop inside. Rather than yelling from the back window, go outside, attract their attention and divert it whenever they bark. Your goal should be to teach them that there are other ways to communicate with you and that their focus should be on you and your home, not whatever is beyond your fence.

Barking is one of the harder things to control in a Belgian Tervuren, largely because of how natural it is for them to do it. However, with proper training, exercise, and attention to what might be causing your Belgian Tervuren's outspoken behavior, that barking can be severely reduced or even stopped.

As a side note, for those considering extreme measures like de-barking surgery, please think twice. The surgery does not actually stop the barking behavior – it just quiets it. Additionally, it is unsafe to ever put an animal under anaesthesia and into surgery, and to do it for cosmetic reasons is unnecessary. If your Belgian Tervuren is barking so much that you're considering a surgery, the odds are that they have a greater, deeper laying fear or anxiety issue that needs to be dealt with anyway. A veterinarian, behaviorist, or Belgian Tervuren trainer can all be more helpful in addressing your concerns than a medical procedure.

5. Chewing

Chewing is another of many built in instinctual actions that a Belgian Tervuren can get caught up in. For many Belgian Tervuren breeds, chewing begins as a Belgian Tervuren, when teething and excess energy get channelled into chewing everything in sight. This is not abnormal, and while it is important to teach a Belgian Tervuren otherwise from a young age, you also need to take precautions, Belgian Tervuren-proofing your home to avoid unnecessary damage.

As your Belgian Tervuren gets older though, chewing can move beyond youthful indiscretion and into the territory of serious behavioral problem – one that needs to be addressed with specific actions and careful training.

Why Do Dogs Chew?

Chewing occurs for a number of reasons, but you should know that it will happen no matter what you do. Your goal should be to direct it toward the right mediums and to minimize it where it can cause destruction. Even then, some dogs may just be psychologically wired to chew more than others. That is when you'll need to make adjustments to their environment to reduce what they have access to.

Retraining a Belgian Tervuren's Instinct to Chew

First, know that most dogs learn their chewing behaviors as

puppies. When teething, they seek out anything in sight to chew on. Owners who give them old socks, shoes, or toys from the house are basically telling them that those items are okay. If your adult Belgian Tervuren is constantly raiding your closet for shoes or old t-shirts, try to remember if you did this when they were young.

Even if you did not give your Belgian Tervuren household items to chew on, you'll need to retrain them to understand that those items are not okay to chew on. Simply yelling at the Belgian Tervuren will almost never have a positive impact. They are doing something natural and until you show them that your belongings are not okay to chew on, the behavior will not stop.

To start, you may consider crate training your Belgian Tervuren. By removing the Belgian Tervuren from an environment as large as your home, you can control what they do when you're not home. To that end, when you are at home, make sure you have a chewing substitute to hand them when they start chewing on a shoe, or a cushion, or whatever else in your home they gravitate towards. A rawhide is often a good substitute if they like leather, fabric, or suede. Some dogs are partial towards rawhide, however, so you may want to take them to the dog store with you and have them choose a chew toy from the racks there.

Deterrents from Chewing

If your Belgian Tervuren continuously finds new things to chew around your home, there are other pro-active ways to stop the chewing behavior. To start with, there are sprays sold by most dog stores that are unpleasant to a Belgian Tervuren when they chew. Bitter apple spray works for many dogs, as does cayenne pepper spray. Make sure to get something organic and non-chemically laden. It should be humane, and just taste bad. You don't want it to cause physical pain.

This kind of deterrent is especially useful for a Belgian Tervuren that has a habit of chewing on cardogs or cushions and clothing. Additionally, you should teach your Belgian Tervuren to "leave it". This common command forces your Belgian Tervuren to drop what they are doing immediately, as you take control of the item. It is an alpha leadership command that is very important for a Belgian Tervuren when you take them out of the house. The last thing you want is a Belgian Tervuren with a home bone or a dead animal in its mouth that will not drop it. The "leave it" command can be taught with treats or a clicker, and a whole lot of patience.

Potential Health Concerns

Something to keep in mind when your Belgian Tervuren chews chronically is that there are certain health conditions that lead a Belgian Tervuren to chew on things like plastic or rubber, or to swallow items whole in place of palatable food. This isn't just a Belgian Tervuren acting out. This is an issue that should be addressed by your vet as it can lead to poisoning or intestinal blockage. If your Belgian Tervuren eats a coin or a rubber band once, you may be able to chalk it up as an accident. If it occurs repeatedly and cannot be curbed with sprays or training, see a vet to learn what options you have.

6. Jumping

Dogs love to jump on things. It is a way of showing their excitement coming to meet someone, and ultimately purging excess energy that they tend to build up. However, it can be dangerous, especially if your Belgian Tervuren is big or if there are small children or elderly people around. The last thing you want is your Belgian Tervuren knocking over your grandmother and breaking a hip or taking down a neighbour's child on accident while trying to play.

Why Dogs Jump

In their world, jumping is a sign of endearment and a way to parlay excitement when someone returns. Puppies will jump up on their mothers when they are young and the mother returns, and as a result, that behavior translates to greeting an owner or a new person to the house that excites them. In some cases dogs will also jump up to exert dominance over another Belgian Tervuren or another person. If you've ever seen a Belgian Tervuren jump onto the back of another Belgian Tervuren's neck, this is what they are doing – showing that Belgian Tervuren that they are superior.

Stopping the Jumping

Jumping can be stopped in a number of ways. However, many

people don't utilise the proper techniques, instead giving their dogs attention they don't need and reinforcing that jumping behavior. Think of it this way. If your Belgian Tervuren were able to talk, they'd be saying "look at me! Dog me! Play with me!" when they jump on you. If you look at them and give them attention, you're doing exactly what they want, effectively rewarding the bad behavior.

So, things like grabbing their paws or pushing them away – while they are effective immediately – will not work in the long run. They'll simply do it again, knowing that additional attention is incoming. When it comes to yelling or showing anger, you'll only confuse your Belgian Tervuren and in some cases, and create potentially dangerous situations when a Belgian Tervuren doesn't know how to greet a stranger to the home.

Properly Ignoring Your Belgian Tervuren

Like many attention seeking behaviors, jumping can be dealt with best by simply ignoring the Belgian Tervuren. Turn away from them and continue about your business. You should not make eye contact, talk to, or touch your Belgian Tervuren for the first few minutes you enter the door. This can be very hard to do, and if you have a family, you'll need to lay down strict rules about how to greet the animal, avoiding that anxious, jumping behavior. For many dogs, that early attention can even breed separation anxiety – causing them to react when you leave or come home.

Of course, you don't need to ignore your Belgian Tervuren forever – just until they relax and stop moving. They might stand patiently waiting, or if they are well trained, they could sit or lay down waiting for your attention. Once they've give you their calm attention, you can reward them softly. Don't get them excited again, but offer them a bit of attention and even a treat if you have any. The goal here is to teach them that your attention will only come when they are calm and patiently waiting for you.

7. Bolting Out the Front Door

One of the scariest things any Belgian Tervuren owner can experience is their Belgian Tervuren getting out the front door without a leash on and attempting to run away. Yet, many Belgian Tervuren owners struggle daily with animals that attempt to do just that. And because dogs are not like cats and have no desire to go anywhere without us, why do they so eagerly burst through the front door whenever it is opened? It is important to not only understand why they do it, but specifically how to stop it to keep your Belgian Tervuren safe and to maintain your peace of mind.

Why Dogs Run out the Door

Dogs run out the door because they don't understand the danger out there. When that door opens, they smell a whole new world – one reminiscent of walks and other animals and a whole number of ways to have fun. It is impossible to tell your Belgian Tervuren that if they go out there, they'll be subject to cars, other animals, your neighbours, and any number of other possible problems that could cause them harm. And, once a Belgian Tervuren has escaped out the door the first time, they'll try repeatedly to do it again – hoping to get that taste of freedom once more.

Setting Household Rules

Before you do anything else, you need to establish clearly stated household rules that will keep your Belgian Tervuren from running out the door before you can properly train him. First, make sure anyone living in the house knows not to open that door until they know where the Belgian Tervuren is and that they are safely beyond range of getting in or out. If someone must hold the Belgian Tervuren until it is possible to safely get in or out, do so.

Second, make sure to communicate these rules to visitors. Other Belgian Tervuren owners without this problem will often assume the Belgian Tervuren won't attempt an escape while non-Belgian Tervuren owners simply don't think about it.

Training Your Belgian Tervuren to Stay Indoors

Of course, no one wants to spend the next 10 years playing footsie with your Belgian Tervuren at the door to keep them from running into the street. So, while the above rules are important and should be established immediately, you should also start training your Belgian Tervuren to stay clear of the door and stop attempting his daring escapes.

Start with the basic commands – sit, stay, and down. These commands are incredibly important for getting and holding your Belgian Tervuren's attention long enough to maintain their position in a single place without running out the door. It will not solve the problem immediately, but to even start the training process, they need to know these commands. As you progress, you'll be teaching your Belgian Tervuren that the door is your territory and that it cannot go near without your specific permission.

Maintaining Position

While teaching a Belgian Tervuren to sit and stay is important, it should go a little further when taking control of the door. Here are some tips to follow:

Introduce a Hand Signal – Along with the "Sit" verbal command, teach your Belgian Tervuren to obey a hand signal, such as an upheld hand, like a crossing guard.

Creating Distance – Choose a line beyond which you don't want your Belgian Tervuren going when you open the door. Have them sit and stay there and then walk toward the door. If they get up at any time, have them sit again before moving.

Holding the Position – If your Belgian Tervuren comes toward the door at all, do not simply have them sit again. Return them to the original position and start from scratch. They need to learn that there is a barrier that they cannot cross and you need to hold steady to it.

Practice – You will need to practice this command repeatedly and enforce it whenever the door is opened. It can be distracting to make guests wait when training your Belgian Tervuren, but it is important to teach the Belgian Tervuren that they need to wait patiently away from the door whenever it is opened.

Make sure, when you are practicing to reward your Belgian Tervuren that they perform the action correctly. If they move forward at all, start over again. But, if you can get to the door, turn the knob and open the door without them reacting, reward them for following your commands.

8. Pulling on the Lead

Walking your Belgian Tervuren should be a relaxing, enjoyable experience – for both of you. Yet, for millions of Belgian Tervuren owners, a walk can be one of the most stressful experiences of the day. An overanxious Belgian Tervuren that pulls on the leash or refuses to listen while out of the house can lead to shortened walks (and less exercise for a hyperactive animal), and ultimately a less enjoyable experience with your dog on a daily basis. Luckily, there are a few simple things you can do to alleviate that constant pulling.

The Walking Relationship

A Belgian Tervuren has an instinctual desire to push back when you push on their chest. By wrapping a collar or harness around them and attaching a leash, you are putting pressure on them that they return in kind. It's an instinctual reaction and it isn't abnormal. But, it can make walking your Belgian Tervuren a painful experience. To avoid this from happening, you need to keep your Belgian Tervuren from putting that pressure on the leash. The more pressure they create, the harder they end up pulling.

As the owner and the holder of the leash, your control over the walking experience is absolute – or it should be. The walk begins the second you pick up the leash, the moment your Belgian Tervuren realizes that they are about to go for a walk. The training to control a pulling Belgian Tervuren must begin at this exact moment – reigning in all that excess energy before it can be transferred into pulling your arm out of its socket.

Starting the Walk

When you start the walk ritual, always have your Belgian Tervuren sit and stay first. You need to put them into a calm-submissive state where their energy is being directed into following your commands. Remember, something as simple as 'sit' and 'stay' takes a serious amount of mental energy and concentration from a Belgian Tervuren – especially when they are that excited. By channeling that energy, you can eliminate the bouncing around that they perform before taking them out. What is important here is that you put the leash away if they exhibit excitement and jumping. Don't reward the behavior.

Once you've attached the leash, make sure the Belgian Tervuren awaits your command entirely. They should not move toward the door or try to pull you in any way until you've given them leave to do so. You should be able to make it to the door without the leash pulling tight. The second the Belgian Tervuren begins to pull, return to the original position and start over again. It can take time to teach a Belgian Tervuren that they cannot pull excitedly, but if you return to that position over and over again, they will get it eventually. Excitement won't get them out the door. The same goes for opening the door. Do it slowly and calmly and stop if the Belgian Tervuren starts to get too excited.

You should never have to punish your Belgian Tervuren. After all, you have the one thing in the world they want most – a walk. By withholding that, you have a powerful reward for them when they finally follow your commands correctly.

Walking Your Belgian Tervuren

Once you finally reach the sidewalk, it is extremely important that you follow the same steps from before. In some cases, it requires that you exhibit even more patience than your Belgian Tervuren, but if you're serious about maintaining the discipline of the walk without being pulled on, you need to make sure the Belgian Tervuren doesn't get rewarded for pulling. Bring a bag of treats with you (or a clicker if you're using that as a training tool) and whenever your Belgian Tervuren properly walks forward at your side with a slack leash, reward them.

If the Belgian Tervuren pulls too hard or starts going in front of you, calmly take a few steps backward and make them sit and stay until you are comfortable moving forward again. Always pull gently on the leash to return to the original positions. Never do anything in anger or put too much force on the leash or the Belgian Tervuren can misinterpret your actions and pull even harder.

It may seem a little abstract, but the goal here is to teach the Belgian Tervuren that when the collar goes tight on their neck, they stop moving. Your voice will not be nearly as effective as that single, sharp physical sensation. It takes longer than many other training exercises, but eventually, your Belgian Tervuren will learn that they don't get to move forward with their walk until the leash is slack. This forces them to walk beside you without pulling and hopefully without too much excitement.

9. Whining

A Belgian Tervuren that whines can be very hard to deal with. The exact causes of the whining are often hard to pinpoint as it is not quite barking, nor is it quite an anxious act. It is simply whining and it can be related to excess energy, separation anxiety, or a desire to reach something they cannot get to. Because the source of whining is hard to pinpoint, it can be hard to stop the behavior, but with these tips it should be easier to narrow down what you need to do and react to it.

Why Do Dogs Whine?

A Belgian Tervuren's whine is very different than a bark, and often times can be harder to stop. It generally means they are in pain or scared, but in many cases it can relate to their being upset about something – often times the result of anxiety.

In domesticated dogs, which are rarely in pain because they are safe indoors, a whine is often a symptom of feeling abandoned by their pack or upset about something in their home. This whine is their way of alarming you to their condition so that you can come and rescue them. Your goal, however, should be to train them to avoid that anxiety.

As a side note, if your Belgian Tervuren never whines or starts whining when nothing apparent is wrong, it very well might be a symptom of pain or illness. If this happens, you should see a vet immediately to have your Belgian Tervuren checked out.

Anxiety Related Whining

When a Belgian Tervuren whines because of separation, it is important to teach your Belgian Tervuren how to accept your absence. If not, that simple whining can advance to damaging and noisy anxiety driven behaviors. In extreme cases, an anxious Belgian Tervuren can destroy your furniture or make messes on the floor when you leave the house. Here are some tips to reduce whining before it becomes full-blown separation anxiety:

Choose Your Belgian Tervuren's Den – Many people will give the Belgian Tervuren the whole house as their territory. This is fine if your Belgian Tervuren is well behaved and doesn't have any problems when you leave. But, if anxiety is an issue, you'll want to consider relegating a single room or a crate for the Belgian Tervuren to inhabit when you leave. By having their own space that they can go to as their "safe spot", they will feel more comfortable when you leave.

Learning to Ignore the Belgian Tervuren at Key Times – Another issue that can create whining in a Belgian Tervuren is giving it too much attention before leaving and when returning. There are two things at play here. When leaving, if you give too much attention, they will feel that separation immediately. When returning home, you will be rewarding whatever anxious behaviors they exhibited when you were gone, teaching them that whining worked to bring you back.

Teaching them to Be Comfortable – To teach your Belgian Tervuren how to be comfortable when you leave, you need to practice doing it while still in the house. With crate training, this can be done simply by putting the Belgian Tervuren in a crate and leaving the room. If you place your Belgian Tervuren in a separate room, the same applies. In many cases, you will need to listen to them whine for a while, but it is important that you don't return to the room before they stop whining. It will only reinforce the behavior.

Not all whining is anxiety related unfortunately. In some cases, it may be just to get attention when you're in the house already. In some cases, this can be a side effect of them having too much nervous energy and not getting enough exercise. In other cases, it may be the result of them trying to get additional attention. In such cases, it is always best to ignore them than to react. If the behavior continues, it could be a sign that you don't have full control of the household and need to do some additional training to assert alpha leadership.

10. Separation Anxiety

A Belgian Tervuren is a very social animal. They live and die in the wild with their pack. In your home, you are their fellow pack members and that means, when they are left alone as you go to work or run errands, they grow anxious and worried that you may not come back. However, just because a Belgian Tervuren is anxious that you are leaving does not mean that they should react so strongly. From barking and whining to destructive behaviors like chewing, digging, and tearing, a Belgian Tervuren with separation anxiety can be very hard to deal with.

The Root of Anxiety

In the wild, a Belgian Tervuren lives and dies through the pack around them. So, it is natural that they see you and your family as their pack. However, in some cases, a Belgian Tervuren may start to panic at the thought of being left alone. They feel as though they are being abandoned, and their survival instincts go a little haywire, causing them to bark, make messes, and even tear things apart as they lose general control of their faculties. When you return home, they might be frantic and unable to control themselves. At first, it might seem like they are very loving, but the messes, destroyed property, and angry calls from neighbours can be stressful for even the most dedicated Belgian Tervuren owner.

Avoiding Separation Anxiety

To start with, you need to rule out the possibility that your Belgian Tervuren is just bored. A Belgian Tervuren that doesn't get enough attention or exercise will often behave in the same way – barking, destroying things, and overreacting when you return home. However, boredom is much easier to fix. It just requires a bit of extra attention and exercise for your Belgian Tervuren. Give them some extra walks, a few toys, and train them with some basic tricks to avoid destruction at unwanted times.

When it comes to anxiety, your Belgian Tervuren's first symptoms will key in on your actions. They can tell when you're about to leave by how you put on your shoes, grab your coat, or pick up your keys. In extreme cases, they will know you're leaving as soon as you wake up, turning them into an utter mess before you even get to the door. To adjust for this, change your routine. Sit down randomly, put on your coat at different times, change when you feed the Belgian Tervuren. The less regular your routines, the harder it is for the Belgian Tervuren to associate them with leaving and the lesser that anxiety will be when you leave.

Solving Existing Anxiety Issues

For many people, anxiety is something that already exists, but it can be resolved before it becomes too destructive. Here are some important tips to help reduce or stop anxiety issues early:

Leaving and Returning Home – When you leave and return home, it is vital that you don't give your Belgian Tervuren too much attention. It can be hard, especially with a new Belgian Tervuren, but that extra attention only highlights for them the fact that you are leaving or were gone. For moderate anxiety, simply ignoring your Belgian Tervuren for a few minutes before you leave and after you return home will reduce their anxiety greatly. For severe cases, other steps will be needed.

Controlling How Long You Are Gone – This is a very complex process and can be hard for anyone that has a regular job and no one else to leave at home. But, it does work well so if your Belgian Tervuren's case is severe enough, consider finding a way to do it. The goal here is to start by leaving your Belgian Tervuren for very short periods of time – only 1-2 minutes or even less if your Belgian Tervuren is extremely anxious. Your goal here should be to only go outside long enough to show your Belgian Tervuren you will return, before their anxiety builds. Don't give the Belgian Tervuren attention when you return. Just keep everything quiet and wait for your Belgian Tervuren to relax. Then, step back outside again and do it all over. Over the course of days, or even weeks, you will increase the time between these sessions, stepping outside for 5 minutes, then 10, then 20, and up to an hour or longer, until you can leave for an entire day and not worry about anxiety.

Consistency – By far the most important thing for a Belgian Tervuren with anxiety is to be consistent with how you handle it. If there are multiple people in the household, they all must ignore the

Belgian Tervuren when returning and leaving. You must maintain the behaviors over time to make them stick.

If things don't click right away, it can take a little time to advance. However, if extreme cases of anxiety persist, you may want to consider talking to a behaviorist or even a vet. There are advanced solutions to this problem, but only if all training attempts are unsuccessful.

A 7-Step Housetraining Guide for Your Belgian Tervuren

Puppies are cuddly, cute and adorable – and at times, extremely gross! You know what I am talking about – when your little darling suddenly presents you with a puddle or pile of urine or feces on your good carpet, it doesn't seem quite so darling then, does it?

Don't feel guilty: It's tough to love a Belgian Tervuren that uses your entire house as its bathroom.

But take heart, you don't have to live with such an individual. You can teach your Belgian Tervuren proper bathroom behavior: to do its business only at the times and only in the places that you want it to. This teaching process is called housetraining and your Belgian Tervuren can ace basic housetraining as long as you follow these seven simple steps.

Step One: Buy a Crate

Years ago, people didn't use crates to housetrain their puppies, and the process was a lot tougher than it is today. Crates tap into a Belgian Tervuren's basic desire to keep its den clean. It'll do anything to avoid pooping or peeing there. That avoidance gives your pup the incentive to develop the bowel and bladder control that's essential to effective housetraining.

In addition to housetraining, your Belgian Tervuren will learn to see the crate as a place to relax and sleep. Right now, though, all you need to know is this: Housetraining is much easier on you and your Belgian Tervuren if you use a crate. Don't try to do it without one.

Here's a tip: In addition to a crate, baby gates can keep your Belgian Tervuren safely confined and help prevent housetraining accidents when you can't watch your Belgian Tervuren.

Step Two: Pick a Potty Spot

Before you can teach your Belgian Tervuren to pee or poop in a specific area, you have to choose the right area best suited to your property. Generally, the best place for that spot is in the backyard near the house. That way, you and your pup won't have to go very far when it needs to poo. Make sure the area is easy to clean; dogs don't like using dirty potties any more than we do.

Another important advantage to using your own property is that you can better protect your Belgian Tervuren from deadly diseases, such as distemper and canine parvovirus. Both diseases can be transmitted through contact with infected Belgian Tervuren's vomit or bodily waste.

Because other dogs – except those that already live with you – aren't likely to eliminate in your yard, your Belgian Tervuren won't come in contact with those potentially disease-transmitting agents.

Step Three: Make Scents

Your Belgian Tervuren's sense of smell is far better than yours. The canine snout has about 220 million cells designed specifically to detect scents, while we humans have only about 5 million such cells. Adding to that incredible scent-detecting capability is the moisture in and on your Belgian Tervuren's nose, which lets it collect large numbers of scent molecules that together amplify what it's already smelling.

Still, another scent-detection enhancement is your Belgian Tervuren's olfactory center (the area of the brain that identifies scents) and nasal membrane, both of which are larger than the corresponding areas in human beings. All of those physiological differences mean that your Belgian Tervuren can detect lots of scents that you cannot.

So what does your Belgian Tervuren's super sniffing mean for your efforts to housetrain it? Quite simply, you can use the scent of a previous bathroom break to show your Belgian Tervuren where you want it to take its next one. The next time your Belgian Tervuren pees, wipe its bottom with a paper towel or soft cloth, and save it.

At the next bathroom break, take the cloth and your Belgian Tervuren to the outdoor potty spot, and place the cloth on the spot. In all likelihood, your Belgian Tervuren will sniff the cloth intently, then re-anoint it. Repeat this process a few times, and soon your

Belgian Tervuren will do its business on the potty spot without the cloth or any other prompting from you.

Step Four: Make a Schedule

Now that you've shown your Belgian Tervuren where you want it to do the doo, you need to show it when you want it to. For a while, though, the timing of its trips to the outdoor potty isn't completely up to you. That's because a Belgian Tervuren can't hold its water – or the other stuff – for very long. In fact, puppies younger than 4 months of age may need 12 to 14 bathroom breaks each day.

The best way to keep track of all those bathroom breaks is to establish pre-determined times when you'll feed your Belgian Tervuren, play with it, take it out and put it in the crate for a nap. Such a schedule not only gives you some predictability during the housetraining process, but your Belgian Tervuren will also become housetrained more quickly. That's because if you take it out to eliminate at the same times every day, its body will become accustomed to the schedule, and it'll be conditioned to do its business when you want it to.

Step Five: Look For Cues, Give One Back

Now that you know how to teach your Belgian Tervuren when

and where to potty, you need to know what to do when it actually eliminates. Once your at the potty spot, you'll see your little doggie sniff the ground intently, perhaps pace or circle, or maybe come to a sudden halt. All of these behaviors are cues that in just a few seconds, your Belgian Tervuren will either produce a puddle or make a deposit.

No matter what your Belgian Tervuren's pre-potty signal is, you need to give it a cue in return as soon as it starts to eliminate. This cue, or potty prompt, should be something like "do your business" or "go potty now." Use the same phrase each time your pup goes, and keep the following point in mind: Make sure you can say the phrase in public.

(Sure, it might be amusing to teach your Belgian Tervuren to pee when you say "take a leak" or "take a whiz," but do you really want to say that out loud in front of strangers? You be the judge.)

It's important to limit your use of the potty cue only to the times you want your Belgian Tervuren to do its business. Some people use a more general phrase, such as "hurry up," but such a choice can backfire. If, for example, your Belgian Tervuren hears you tell your child to "hurry up" and get out the door to school, your Belgian Tervuren may present you with a most unwelcome gift.

Eventually, your Belgian Tervuren may associate the phrase with the deed, and potty exactly when you tell it to. Such skills come in handy on cold or rainy nights when you have to take your Belgian Tervuren out for a potty break, but you don't want to have to wait too long for it to unload.

In any case, once your Belgian Tervuren finishes its business, praise the pup lavishly and give it a small treat. Then, bring it back inside. Potty time shouldn't turn into play time.

Step Six: Be Vigilant

While your Belgian Tervuren is still learning the housetraining basics, your job is to make sure that it doesn't have the opportunity to make mistakes (or at least as few as possible). For this reason, when your pup is not in its crate, you must watch it carefully. In fact, don't take your eyes off it.

If your pup shows any signs that it needs to potty, scoop it up into your arms and get it outside. Then, when your Belgian Tervuren eliminates, praise it enthusiastically. If you're too late, and your Belgian Tervuren graces your carpet with a puddle or deposit, put your Belgian Tervuren in its crate and clean up the mess without comment.

Use an enzymatic cleaner designed specifically for dog stains to eliminate the odors that might encourage your Belgian Tervuren to potty at that spot again. Then, promise yourself and your Belgian Tervuren that you'll keep a closer eye on it in the future to prevent such an accident from happening again.

Step Seven: Be Patient

And finally, have patience. Don't expect your Belgian Tervuren to learn its bathroom manners overnight. Housetraining takes time, patience and understanding. Your Belgian Tervuren needs time not only to figure out what you want it to do, but also to develop the physical ability to control its urges to poop or pee until it gets to the potty place.

Conclusion

Your Belgian Tervuren is a good Belgian Tervuren – however they may act right now. They just need to be given the tools and the support from their owner needed to overcome unwanted behaviors. That's where you come in. As the owner and de facto pack leader of your home, it is your duty to give your Belgian Tervuren structure, providing them with the rules to live by that all animals need.

By giving your Belgian Tervuren that leadership, as well as stimulating them intellectually and wearing them out physically, you will be surprised by just how many behaviors on this list will slowly (or not so slowly) disappear for good.

But, even if the behaviors don't disappear overnight, it is important to be persistent and consistent. Your Belgian Tervuren may not learn immediately, but when it finally sinks in and they understand that they cannot chew on your TV remote or pee in the front hallway, they will likely remember that for the rest of their lives, striving on a daily basis to make their owner happy and to follow the boundaries you have set for them.

It all starts with you and a desire to have a happier, more wholesome relationship with your Belgian Tervuren. If you're ready, you can bet your canine friend is as well.

Made in the USA
Las Vegas, NV
13 May 2024

89890093R00046